The Sa

The Sayings of the Buddha
The Sayings of Jesus
The Sayings of Moses
The Sayings of Muhammad

The Sayings of

THE BIBLE

Selected by

MICHAEL GRANT

THE ECCO PRESS

THE ECCO PRESS
100 West Broad Street
Hopewell, New Jersey 08525

Published simultaneously in Canada by
Penguin Books Canada Ltd., Ontario
Printed in the United States of America

Library of Congress Cataloging-in-Publication Data
Bible.   English, New King James.   Selections.   1998.
    The sayings of the Bible / selected by Michael Grant. — 1st Ecco Press ed.
        p.   cm.
    Originally published: London : Duckworth, 1994.
    ISBN 0-88001-639-6
    1. Bible—Quotations.   I. Grant, Michael, 1914-   II. Title.
BS432.B4465   1998
220.5'2036—dc21   98-4040
                                                                        CIP

9 8 7 6 5 4 3 2 1

FIRST EDITION 1998

Contents

PART II THE NEW TESTAMENT

Introduction

How many people have read the Bible? Very few. Yet if we were stranded on a desert island, and only allowed one book, we should be very foolish if we did not choose the Bible as that book. For it contains enough to keep us busy and thoughtful for a lifetime. In fact, however, to call it a 'book' is misleading, since it is not a single book but an entire, amazing library (*biblia*, books). It was composed over a period of many centuries in Hebrew, Aramaic and Greek. Some of its authors were very learned, others were not. Its contents are extremely varied, but its subject is one: the glorification of God. This it achieves by narrative, but also by extremely articulate and memorable sayings.

Three-quarters of what Christians regard as the Bible today comprises the Hebrew scriptures, known from early Christian times as the Old Testament. The basic theme of the Old Testament is God's relationship with his chosen people the Jews, although the stories of the Creation and the visions of the prophets make it clear that this theme is seen within the context of the ultimate redemption of all humankind.

This Hebrew Bible, our Old Testament, is subdivided into the Torah or Pentateuch, the Prophets and the Sacred Writings (Hagiographa). The books of the Torah are Genesis, Exodus, Leviticus, Numbers and Deuteronomy. The books of the Prophets include the historical books or 'former prophets' (Joshua, Judges, I and II Samuel and I and II Kings), and the 'latter prophets', classified according to length as 'major' (Isaiah, Jeremiah and Ezekiel) and 'minor' or 'the twelve' (Hosea, Joel, Amos, Obadiah, Jonah, Micah, Nahum, Habakkuk, Zephaniah, Haggai, Zechariah, Malachi). The

Sacred Writings comprise (1) the Psalms, Proverbs, Job; (2) The Scrolls or Megilloth (Song of Solomon, Ruth, Lamentations, Ecclesiastes, Esther); (3) Daniel, Ezra, Nehemiah and I and II Chronicles.

The authorships (sometimes composite) and dates of these various books are often highly controversial. Some of the earliest stories are very early indeed. As for the dates of the principal events, the Exodus of the Jews from Egypt seems to have occurred, not necessarily all at once, some time after 1300 BC. David's reign is attributed to *c*. 1000-965 BC and Solomon's to *c*. 965-927 BC. The northern kingdom of Israel fell to the Assyrians in 722/1 BC and the southern kingdom of Judah to the Babylonians in 587 BC. Subsequently the Jews came under the Ptolemies and the Seleucids (successor states of Alexander the Great) and their own Maccabean dynasty. Ecclesiasticus was probably composed in classical Hebrew by Ben Sira (Sirach) in 190-180 BC and translated into Greek by his grandson in 132 BC.

This vast period is not covered systematically, but with a view to describing the ways of God in his relations with the Jews. *Genesis* deals with the beginnings of the Universe and the human race, followed by Adam and Eve's fall into sin. Then comes the Flood survived by Noah, and Abraham inaugurates the covenant of God with himself and his descendants, his son Isaac, Isaac's son Jacob, and the tribes of Israel. *Exodus* recounts the deliverance from Egypt under the leadership of Moses, to whom God gives the law on Mount Sinai, despite the idolatry of the people, and his prescriptions for worship are continued in *Leviticus*. *Numbers* carries the people on through forty years of wandering in the wilderness, and prepares the way for the conquest of Canaan (Palestine), which is told in *Joshua*, with references to God's forgiveness for their frequent ingratitude. *Deuteronomy*, filled with Moses' discourses, rehearses the events that have brought the

Israelites within sight of their Promised Land.

Joshua tells how the people conquered that land, and *Judges* describes their situation at that juncture. *I Samuel* begins with the career of Samuel as a prelude to the monarchy. He anoints Saul as the first king, and *II Samuel* describes the life and character of his successor David. *I* and *II Kings* outline the glory and partial apostasy of Solomon, after whose death the nation is divided into the two kingdoms of Israel and Judah, notable for the prophetic lives of Elijah and Elisha. The most influential of the prophetic writers is *Isaiah,* or rather the two writers who composed the book that goes under his name. The second writer, after the sack of Jerusalem by the Babylonians, ascribes future salvation to God's Suffering Servant. But *Jeremiah,* above all, is the voice of doom for this kingdom of Judah. *Ezekiel,* by means of visions, comforts the people in their affliction. The twelve 'minor' prophets provide many additional commentaries on the history of Israel and Judah, which they interpret as a sign of God's judgment and mercy.

Job, Psalms and *Proverbs* constitute the principal poetic literature of the Old Testament. *Job* grapples, in the most thought-provoking sophisticated fashion, with the problem of evil, and why it often prevails, despite the supposedly supreme power of God. The *Psalms* contain poems and hymns of all periods which express various forms of devotion to him. *Proverbs* turns away from Israel's history and offers acute general maxims about life. The Scrolls or Megilloth include the *Song of Songs* (Solomon), a series of torrid love poems which earned their inclusion in the Bible from the belief that they were allegories (composed by the King) of the love between God and Israel. *Ruth* was a foreign, Moabite woman who married an Israelite and became an ancestress of David. *Lamentations* is a series of mournful acrostics. *Ecclesiastes,* by 'the Preacher', is clever, disillusioned 'Wisdom Literature'.[1] *Esther* was the Jewish wife of the

Persian king Ahasuerus (Xerxes I, 436–465 BC). *Daniel* is a dramatic tale of God's interventions to save the hero. *I* and *II Chronicles* supplement *Kings*. *Ezra* tells of the return of the Jews from Babylonian captivity, and *Nehemiah*, closely related, describes the reconstruction of Jerusalem's city walls.

Then follows that ambiguous category of the Books of the Apocrypha, 'hidden away', either in a literal sense or, more probably, because they were deemed unsuitable for general circulation. They appeared in the Septuagint translation of the Old Testament into Greek, but not in the Hebrew text, and in Catholic but not Protestant versions of the scriptures. They include additions to three Old Testament works, but are made up chiefly of seven books. The first is *Tobit*, which tells his story and that of Sarah, each of whom turned to God after suffering anguish. *Judith* was a beautiful Jewish widow who tricked the Assyrian general Holofernes. *The Wisdom of Solomon*, like *Proverbs*, traces the origin of wisdom to God. *Ecclesiasticus*, 'the Wisdom of Jesus the Son of Sirach', provides an exceptionally rich assortment of pungent sayings, upholding the moral aspects of the Torah and the accountability of God's people, and stressing the divine retribution that is visited on the wicked – which *Job* and *Ecclesiastes* had doubted. *Baruch* supplements its praise of divine wisdom by poems. *I* and *II Maccabees* relate the struggles of the Jews against subordination to the Seleucids, the imperial state which controlled Judaea.

The New Testament is the Christian addition to the Old Testament. It deals with the life of Jesus Christ and its aftermath, and at its very centre is the theme of the Kingship (Kingdom) of God or Heaven, which would be realised at the end of the world and would mean the accomplishment of his will upon earth. John the Baptist proclaimed that the establishment of the Kingdom was imminent, and it seemed that Jesus had begun to bring it in – insisting that, by God's order, he was able to forgive sins, which appeared to the Jews a blasphemy against monotheism – although it would not be fully realised until a little later on. Jesus' incomparably brilliant and attractive preaching was directed mainly to the Jews (although his contacts with non-Jews would have been extended if he had lived), but Paul deliberately designed his message for the entire Gentile world.

The Four Gospels attributed to *Matthew, Mark, Luke* and *John* – none of which, apparently, are less than several decades later than the death of Jesus (*c.* AD 30/36)[2] – deal in various different fashions with the life, person and teachings of Jesus, as the Christian Community remembered them. *Acts,* written as a continuation of Luke's Gospel, carries the story of Christianity from the resurrection of Jesus to the end of the career of Paul. But we also have a number of Paul's own letters, which are intensely important because of their early date (from *c.* AD 50),[3] and the overwhelming personality of their author, his unique capacity to express himself, and his gigantic contribution to the subsequent history of the church. Out of the twenty-one Letters which comprise by far the largest number of writings in the New Testament, more than half are ascribed to Paul. *Romans* has the most complete statement of his teachings. *I* and *II Corinthians* reveal many of the problems that afflicted early Christian communities. *Galatians* distinguishes with particular sharpness between the Gospel and Jewish Law, which Paul, although a Jew by birth, came to reject as useless, believing that the crucifixion, resurrection and ascension of Jesus had introduced a completely new epoch, preparing the way for the imminent Kingdom of God. The last book of the Bible, the *Revelation of St John the Divine,* or Apocalypse, consists of a series of visions granted to the unknown writer (towards the end of the first century), and communicated by him to church congregations in Asia Minor.

All the books of the New Testament are determined manifestations of 'typology', interpreting texts in the Old Testament as predicting and prefiguring subsequent events, notably the career, sayings, death and resurrection of Jesus. This is because the books of the New Testament were composed not merely to satisfy historical curiosity about the happenings they profess to describe, but to bear witness to faith in the action of God through those events, action which, it was believed, the Old Testament had prophesied. We may perhaps accept none of this, but we cannot fail, all the same, to be impressed by the unerring force of many of the sayings which are enshrined in both Testaments, Old and New.

Translations are from the Authorised Version of King James I of England and VI of Scotland (1611), with occasional additions from the New English Bible (1961, 1970), when these are notably different. (See also the Revised English Bible, 1982, 1990.)

PART I

THE OLD TESTAMENT AND APOCRYPHA

God

And God said unto Moses: I am that I am.[4]

Exodus 3.14

And mount Sinai was altogether on a smoke, because the Lord descended upon it in fire: and the smoke thereof ascended as the smoke of a furnace, and the whole mount quaked greatly. And when the voice of the trumpet sounded long, and waxed louder and louder, Moses spake, and God answered him by a voice ... And the Lord called Moses up to the top of the mount; and Moses went up. And the Lord said unto Moses, Go down, charge the people, lest they break through unto the Lord to gaze, and many of them perish.

Exodus 19.18,21

Ye shall make you no idols nor graven image, neither rear you up a standing image, neither shall ye set up any image of stone in your land to bow down unto it: for I am the Lord your God.

Leviticus 26.1

Hear, O Israel: The Lord our God is One God ... the Lord thy God is a jealous God.

Deuteronomy 6.4,15

And, behold, the Lord passed by, and a great and strong wind rent the mountains, and brake in pieces the rocks before the Lord. But the Lord was not in the wind. And after the wind an earthquake. But the Lord was not in the earthquake. And after the earthquake a fire. But the Lord was not in the fire. And after the fire a still small voice. And it was so, when Elijah heard it, that he wrapped his face in his mantle, and went out, and stood in the entering in of the cave. And, behold, there came a voice unto him, and said, What doest thou here, Elijah?

I Kings 19.11-13

Then Job answered and said ... How should man be just with God? If he will contend with him he cannot answer him one of a thousand. Job 9.1,3

Then answered Zophar the Naamathite [to Job] ... Canst thou by searching find out God?

Job 11.1,7

Then the Lord answered Job out of the whirlwind, and said ... Where wast thou when I laid the foundations of the earth? Declare, if thou hast understanding!

Job 38.1,4

Hast thou an arm like God? Or canst thou thunder with a voice like him?

Job 40.9

Then Job answered the Lord, and said, I know that thou canst do everything, and that no thought can be withholden from thee ... Wherefore I abhor myself, and repent in dust and ashes.

Job 42.1,2,6

How long will thou forget me, O Lord? For ever? How long wilt thou hide thy face from me?

Psalms 13.1

The Lord is my shepherd: I shall not want. He maketh me to lie down in green pastures. He leadeth me beside the still waters.

Psalms 23.1,2

As the heart panteth after the water brooks, so panteth my soul after thee, O God. My soul thirsteth for God, for the living God. When shall I come and appear before God? Psalms 42.1,2

They that go down to the sea in ships, that do business in great waters: these see the works of the Lord, and his wonders in the deep ... O that men would praise the Lord for his goodness, and for his wonderful works to the children of men! Psalms 107.23,24,31

Except the Lord build the house, they labour in vain that build it. Psalms 127.1

O Lord, thou hast searched me, and known me. Thou knowest my downsitting and mine uprising, thou understandest my thought afar off.
Psalms 139.1,2

He hath made the earth by his power, he hath established the world by his wisdom, and hath stretched out the heaven by his understanding.[5]
Jeremiah 51.15

Surely vain are all men by nature, who are ignorant of God, and could not out of the good things that are seen know him that is: neither by acknowledging the works did they acknowledge the workmaster.
Wisdom of Solomon 13.1

Look at the generations of old, and see: Did ever any trust in the Lord, and was confounded? Or did any abide in his fear, and was forsaken? Or whom did he ever despise, that called upon him?
Ecclesiasticus 2.10

We may speak much, and yet come short. Wherefore in sum, he is all. Ecclesiasticus 43.27

O all ye that worship the Lord, bless the God of gods, praise him and give him thanks: for his mercy endureth for ever.
Song of the Three (Children) (Apocrypha) 68

The Early Legends

And God said, Let us make man in our image, after our likeness.

Genesis 1.26

But of the tree of the knowledge of good and evil, thou shalt not eat of it: for in the day that thou eatest thereof thou shalt surely die.

Genesis 2.17

And the eyes of them both [Adam and Eve] were opened, and they knew that they were naked: and they sewed fig leaves together, and made themselves aprons.

Genesis 3.7

And the Lord God said, Behold, the man is become as one of us, to know good and evil: and now, lest he put forth his hand, and take also of the tree of life, and eat, and live for ever: therefore the Lord God sent him forth from the garden of Eden, to till the ground from whence he was taken. So he drove out the man.

Genesis 3.22-24

Cain [the son of Adam and Eve] rose up against Abel his brother, and slew him. And the Lord said unto Cain, Where is Abel thy brother? And he said: I know not. Am I my brother's keeper? And he said: What hast thou done? The voice of thy brother's blood crieth unto me from the ground. And now art thou cursed from the earth, which hath opened her mouth to receive thy brother's blood from thy hand.

Genesis 4.8-11

And behold I, even I, do bring a flood of waters upon the earth, to destroy all flesh, wherein is the breath of life, from under heaven: and everything that is in the earth shall die. But with thee [Noah] will I establish my covenant: and thou shalt come into the ark, thou and thy sons, and thy wife, and thy son's wives with thee.

Genesis 6.17-18

And Abraham bound Isaac his son, and laid him on the altar upon the wood. And Abraham stretched forth his hand, and took the knife to slay his son. And the angel of the Lord called unto him out of heaven, and said, Abraham, Abraham. And he said, Here am I. And he said, Lay not thine hand upon the lad, neither do thou anything unto him; for now I know that thou fearest God, seeing thou hast not withheld thy son, thine only son, from me. And Abraham lifted up his eyes, and looked, and behold behind him a ram caught in a thicket by his horns. And Abraham went and took the ram, and offered him up for a burnt offering in the stead of his son.

Genesis 22.9-13

And when she [Jochebed, the daughter of Levi] could no longer hide him [Moses] she took for him an ark of bulrushes, and daubed it with slime and with pitch, and put the child therein: and she laid it in the flags by the river's edge [6] ... And the daughter of Pharaoh came down to wash herself at the river: and her maidens walked along by the river's side; and when she saw the ark among the flags, she sent her maid to fetch it. And when she had opened it, she saw the child: and, behold, the babe wept. And she had compassion on him, and said: This is one of the Hebrews' children.

Exodus 2.3,5-6

And the angel of the Lord appeared unto him in a flame of fire out of the midst of a bush: and he looked, and, behold, the bush burned with fire, and the bush was not consumed. And Moses said, I will now turn aside, and see this great sight, why the bush is not burnt. And when the Lord saw that he turned aside to see, God called unto him out of the midst of the bush, and said, Moses, Moses. And he said, Here am I.   Exodus 3.2-4

Get thee unto Pharaoh … saying, Let my people go.

Exodus 7.16

And the Lord said unto Moses, Stretch out thine hand over the sea, that the waters may come again upon the Egyptians, upon their chariots, and upon their horsemen. And Moses stretched forth his hand over the sea, and the sea returned to his strength when the morning appeared: and the Egyptians fled against it: and the Lord overthrew the Egyptians in the midst of the sea.

Exodus 14.26-27

And it came to pass at the seventh time, when the priests blew with the trumpets, Joshua said unto the people, Shout! For the Lord hath given you the city [Jericho][7] … So the people shouted when the priests blew with the trumpets: and it came to pass, when the people heard the sound of the trumpet, and the people shouted with a great shout, that the wall fell down flat, so that the people went up into the city, every man straight before him, and they took the city. And they utterly destroyed all that was in the city.

Joshua 6.16,20-21

The Chosen People &
Promised Land

Now the Lord had said unto Abram [Abraham], Get thee out of thy country, and from thy kindred, and from thy father's house, unto a land that I will show thee. And I will make of thee a great nation.   Genesis 12.1-2

The Lord made a covenant with Abram, saying, Unto thy seed have I given this land, from the river of Egypt unto the great river, the river Euphrates.   Genesis 15.18

I am the Lord God of Abraham thy father, and the God of Isaac: the land whereon thou [Jacob] liest, to thee will I give it, and to thy seed. And thy seed shall be as the dust of the earth, and thou shalt spread abroad to the west, and to the east, and to the north, and to the south.
                                                    Genesis 28.13-14

Now therefore, if ye will obey my voice indeed, and keep my covenant, then ye shall be a peculiar treasure unto me above all people: for all the earth is mine. And ye shall be unto me a kingdom of priests, and a holy nation.   Exodus 19.5

All the commandments which I command thee this day shall ye observe to do, that ye may live, and multiply, and go in and possess the land which the Lord sware unto your fathers.   Deuteronomy 8.1

Behold the land of Canaan [Palestine], which I give unto the children of Israel for a possession.   Deuteronomy 32.49

Behold, he that keepeth Israel shall neither slumber nor sleep.   Psalms 121.4

The days of the life of man may be numbered: but the days of Israel are innumerable.   Ecclesiasticus 37.25

The Law

And the Lord said unto Moses, Come up to me into the mount, and be there: and I will give thee tables of stone, and a Law, and commandments which I have written: that thou mayest teach them.

Exodus 24.12

The proud have forged a lie against me: but I will keep thy precepts with my whole heart. Their heart is as fat as grease: but I delight in thy Law ... Let thy tender mercies come unto me, that I may live: for thy Law is my delight ... O how I love thy Law! It is my meditation all the day ... I hate and abhor lying: but thy Law do I love ... Great peace have they which love thy law: and nothing shall offend them.

Psalms 119.69-70,77,97,163,165

Let us hear the conclusion of the whole matter. Fear God, and keep his commandments. For this is the whole duty of man.

Ecclesiastes 12.13

They that love him shall be filled with the Law.

Ecclesiasticus 2.16

Let thy mind be upon the ordinances of the Lord, and meditate continually in his commandments.

Ecclesiasticus 6.37

He that hath the knowledge of the Law shall obtain her [wisdom].

Ecclesiasticus 15.1

The Prophets

Then said Elijah unto the people, I, even I only, remain a prophet of the Lord: but the prophets of Baal[8] are four-hundred and fifty men.   I Kings 18.22

And he [King Ahaziah of Israel, *c.* 852-1 BC] said unto them, What manner of man was he which came up to meet you, and told you these words? And they answered him, He was a hairy man, and girt with a girdle of leather about his loins. And he said, It is Elijah the Tishbite.   II Kings 1.7-8

And he [Elisha] took the mantle of Elijah that fell from him, and smote the waters, and said, Where is the Lord God of Elijah? And when he also had smitten the waters, they parted hither and thither: and Elisha went over.
                    II Kings 2.14

Also I heard the voice of the Lord, saying: Whom shall I send, and who will go for us? Then said I, Here am I; send me.   Isaiah 6.8

For unto us a child is born, unto us a son is given … He is despised and rejected of men … He is brought as a lamb to the slaughter … He was taken from prison and from judgment.[9]   Isaiah 9.6; 53.3,7-8

Then said I, Ah, Lord God! Behold, I cannot speak. For I am a child. But the Lord said unto me, Say not I am a child. For thou shalt go to all that I shall send thee, and whatsoever I command thee thou shalt speak.
                    Jeremiah 1.6-7

And he said unto me, Son of Man,[10] stand upon thy feet, and I will speak to thee. And the spirit entered into me when he spake unto me, and set me upon my feet, that I heard him that spake unto me.   Ezekiel 2.1-2

Foreigners & Unbelievers

And he [Noah] said, Cursed be Canaan: a servant of
servants shall he be unto his brethren.   Genesis 9.25

And the Lord spake unto Moses, saying: Avenge the
children of Israel of the Midianites.[11]

Numbers 31.1-2

Then said Joshua, Open the mouth of the cave, and bring
out those five kings unto me out of the cave … And
afterward Joshua smote them and slew them, and
hanged them on five trees: and they were hanging up on
the trees until the evening.   Joshua 10.22,26

Then she [Ruth the Moabite] fell on her face, and bowed
herself to the ground, and said unto him [Boaz][12], Why
have I found grace in thine eyes, that thou shouldst take
knowledge of me, seeing I am a stranger?

Ruth 2.10

Then said David to the Philistine [Goliath], Thou comest
to me with a sword, and with a spear, and with a shield:
but I come to thee in the name of the Lord of Hosts, the
God of the armies of Israel, whom thou hast defied …
And David put his hand in his bag, and took thence a
stone, and slang it, and smote the Philistine in his
forehead, that the stone sunk into his forehead: and he
fell upon his face to the earth.

I Samuel 17.45,49

Thou shalt break them [the heathen] with a rod of iron:
thou shalt dash them in pieces like a potter's vessel.

Psalms 2.9

Arise, O Lord: save me, O my God: for thou hast smitten
all my enemies upon the cheekbone: thou hast broken
the teeth of the ungodly.

Psalms 3.7

Then she [Judith] approached to his [Holofernes'] bed,[13] and took hold of the hair of his head, and said, Strengthen me, O Lord God of Israel, this day! And she smote twice upon his neck with all her might, and she took away his head from him.

Judith 13.7-8

Vengeance

Whoso sheddeth man's blood by man shall his blood be shed.
Genesis 9.6

To me belongeth vengeance, and recompence: their foot shall slide in due time.
Deuteronomy 32.35

O Lord God, to whom vengeance belongeth: O God, to whom vengeance belongeth, show thyself.
Psalms 94.1

Say not, I will do so to him as he hath done to me.
Proverbs 24.29

If thine enemy be hungry, give him bread to eat: and if he be thirsty, give him water to drink. For thou shalt heap coals of fire upon his head, and the Lord shall reward thee.
Proverbs 25.21

Thus saith the Lord ... Flee out of the midst of Babylon, and deliver every man his soul: be not cut off in her iniquity: for this is the time of the Lord's vengeance: he will render unto her a recompence.
Jeremiah 51.1,6

I will lay my vengeance upon Edom[14] by the hand of my people Israel ... and they shall know my vengeance, saith the Lord God ... I will execute great vengeance upon them [the Philistines] with furious rebukes.
Ezekiel 25.14,17

The book of the vision of Nahum the Elkoshite. God is jealous, and the Lord revengeth: the Lord revengeth, and is furious: the Lord will take vengeance on his adversaries, and he reserveth wrath for his enemies.
Nahum 1.2

Good & Evil

Honour thy father and thy mother: that thy days may be long upon the land which the Lord thy God giveth thee. Thou shalt not kill. Thou shalt not commit adultery. Thou shalt not steal. Thou shalt not bear false witness against thy neighbour. Thou shalt not covet thy neighbour's house, thou shalt not covet thy neighbour's wife, nor his manservant, nor his maidservant, nor his ox, nor his ass, nor anything that is thy neighbour's.[15]

Exodus 20.12-17

But there was none like unto Ahab,[16] which did sell himself to work wickedness in the sight of the Lord, whom Jezebel his wife stirred up.

I Kings 21.25

This is one thing, therefore I said it: He destroyeth the perfect and the wicked ... The earth is given into the hand of the wicked ... If I be wicked, woe unto me. And if I be righteous, yet will I not lift up my head. I am full of confusion.

Job 9.22,24; 10.15

Wherefore do the wicked live, become old, yea, are mighty in power?

Job 21.7

I was envious at the foolish, when I saw the prosperity of the wicked ... Until I went into the sanctuary of God: then understood I their end. Surely thou didst set them in slippery places: thou castedst them down into destruction.

Psalms 73.3,17-18

Lord, how long shall the wicked, how long shall the wicked triumph?

Psalms 94.3

The upright shall dwell in the land, and the perfect shall remain in it. But the wicked shall be cut off from the earth, and the transgressors shall be rooted out of it.

Proverbs 2.21-22

Better is a little with righteousness than great revenues without right.

Proverbs 16.8

One that returneth from righteousness to sin: the Lord prepareth such a one for the sword.

Ecclesiasticus 26.28

Women

And the Lord God said, It is not good that the man should be alone: I will make him a help meet for him ... And Adam said, Therefore shall a man leave his father and mother, and shall cleave unto his wife: and they shall be one flesh.

Genesis 2.18,23,24

And Jezebel his wife said unto him [Ahab], Dost thou now govern the kingdom of Israel? Arise, and eat bread, and let thine heart be merry: I will give thee the vineyard of Naboth the Jezreelite. So she wrote letters in Ahab's name, and sealed them with his seal ...

I Kings 21.7-8

Such is the way of an adulterous woman: she eateth, and wipeth her mouth, and saith, I have done no wickedness.

Proverbs 30.20

Who can find a virtuous woman? For her price is far above rubies.

Proverbs 31.10

How beautiful are thy feet with shoes,[17] O prince's daughter. The joints of thy thighs are like jewels, the work of the hands of a cunning workman. Thy navel is like a round goblet, which wanteth not liquor.[18] Thy belly is like an heap of wheat set about with lilies. Thy two breasts are like two young roes which are twins.

Song of Songs (Solomon) 7.1-3

Forego not a wise and good woman: for her grace is above gold ... Hast thou a wife after thy mind? Forsake her not: but give not thyself over to a light woman.

Ecclesiasticus 7.19,26

Hast thou daughters? Have a care of their body, and show not thyself cheerful toward them. Marry thy daughter, and so shalt thou have performed a weighty matter; but give her to a man of understanding.

Ecclesiasticus 7.24-25

Be not jealous over the wife of thy bosom, and teach her not an evil lesson against thyself.

Ecclesiasticus 9.1

Give not thy soul unto a woman to set her foot upon thy substance.

Ecclesiasticus 9.2

Give not thy soul unto harlots, that thou lose not thine inheritance. Look not round about thee in the streets of the city, neither wander thou in the solitary places thereof.

Ecclesiasticus 9.6-7

Sit not at all with another man's wife, nor sit down with her in thine arms, and spend not thy money with her at the wine: lest thine heart incline unto her, and so through thy desire thou fall into destruction.

Ecclesiasticus 9.9

All bread is sweet to a whoremonger: he will not leave off till he die.

Ecclesiasticus 23.17

Give me any plague, but the plague of the heart! And any wickedness, but the wickedness of a woman!

Ecclesiasticus 25.13

If there be kindness, meekness and comfort in her tongue, then is not her husband like other men.

Ecclesiasticus 36.23

Friendship

And it came to pass ... that the soul of Jonathan was knit
with the soul of David, and Jonathan loved him as his
own soul. And David lamented with this lamentation
over Saul and over Jonathan his son: Saul and Jonathan
were lovely and pleasant in their lives, and in their
deaths they were not divided: they were swifter than
eagles, they were stronger than lions ... I am distressed
for thee, my brother Jonathan: very pleasant hast thou
been unto me: thy love to me was wonderful, passing
the love of women.

I Samuel 18.1; II Samuel 1.23,26

The poor is hated even of his own neighbour: but the
rich hath many friends.

Proverbs 14.20

He that repeateth a matter separateth friends.

Proverbs 17.9

Be in peace with many: nevertheless have but one
counsellor of a thousand. If thou wouldst get a friend,
prove him first, and be not hasty to credit him. For some
man is a friend for his own occasion, and will not abide
in the day of thy trouble.

Ecclesiasticus 6.6-8

Every friend saith, I am his friend also. But there is a
friend which is only a friend in name ... Consult not
with one that suspecteth thee: and hide thy counsel from
such as envy thee.

Ecclesiasticus 37.1,10

Tact & Discretion

Then Job answered the Lord, and said, Behold, I am vile: what shall I answer thee? I will lay mine hand upon my mouth. Once have I spoken; but I will not answer: yea, twice: but I will proceed no further.

Job 40.4-5

I will keep my mouth with a bridle, while the wicked is before me.

Psalms 39.1

Strive not with a man without cause, if he have done thee no harm.

Proverbs 3.30

Reprove not a scorner, lest he hate thee: rebuke a wise man, and he will love thee.

Proverbs 9.8

He that refraineth his lips is wise ... A talebearer revealeth secrets: but he that is of a faithful spirit concealeth the matter.

Proverbs 10.19; 11.13

A soft answer turneth away wrath: but grievous words stir up anger ... pleasant words are as a honeycomb, sweet to the soul, and health to the bones.

Proverbs 15.1; 16.24

A fool's mouth is his destruction, and his lips are the snare of his soul ... The words of a talebearer are as wounds, and they go down into the innermost parts of the belly.

Proverbs 18.7-8

Be not rash with thy mouth ... Let thy words be few ... The lips of a fool will swallow up himself.

Ecclesiastes 5.2; 10.12

Sweet language will multiply friends.

Ecclesiasticus 6.5

Open not thine heart to every man, lest he requite thee with a shrewd turn.

Ecclesiasticus 8.19

Answer not before thou hast heard the cause: neither interrupt men in the midst of their talk.

Ecclesiasticus 11.8

He that hateth babblings shall have less evil.

Ecclesiasticus 19.6

Wine

And Noah began to be a husbandman, and he planted a vineyard. And he drank of the wine, and was drunken; and he was uncovered within his tent.[19]

Genesis 9.20,21

Wine is a mocker, strong drink is raging.

Proverbs 20.1

Look not thou upon the wine when it is red, when it giveth his colour in the cup ... At the last it biteth like a serpent, and stingeth like an adder.

Proverbs 23.31

Wine maketh merry: but money answereth all things.

Ecclesiastes 10.19

Stay me with flagons, comfort me with apples: for I am sick with love.

Song of Songs (Solomon) 2.5

Woe unto them that rise up early in the morning, that they may follow strong drink.

Isaiah 5.11

They shall not drink wine with a song: strong drink shall be bitter to them that drink it.

Isaiah 24.9

Wine is as good as life to a man, if it be drunk moderately. What life is then to a man that is without wine? For it was made to make men glad.

Ecclesiasticus 2.27

Shocks & Surprises

And he [Jacob] came unto his father [Isaac], and said, My father: and he said, Here am I: who art thou, my son? And Jacob said unto his father, I am Esau thy firstborn;[20] I have done according as thou badest me: arise, I pray thee, sit and eat of my venison, that thy soul may bless me.

Genesis 27.18-19

And it came to pass in the morning, that David wrote a letter to Joab, and sent it by the hand of Uriah.[21] And he wrote in the letter, saying: Set ye Uriah in the forefront of the hottest battle, and retire ye from him, that he may be smitten and die.

II Samuel 11.14-15

And Elijah said unto them, Take the prophets of Baal: let not one of them escape. And they took them: and Elijah brought them down to the brook Kishon, and slew them there.

I Kings 18.40

And he [Elisha] went up from thence unto Beth-el:[22] and as he was going up by the way, there came forth little children out of the city and mocked him, and said unto him, Go up, thou bald head; go up, thou bald head. And he turned back, and looked on them, and cursed them in the name of the Lord. And there came forth two she-bears out of the wood, and tare forty and two children of them.

II Kings 2.23-24

Famous Epigrams & Bywords

And God said, Let there be light. And there was light.
Genesis 1.3

And the Lord set a mark upon Cain.
Genesis 4.15

The stars in their courses fought against Sisera.[23]
Judges 5.20

And she named the child Ichabod, saying, The glory is departed from Israel ... for the ark of God is taken.
I Samuel 4.21-22

And all the people shouted and said, God save the king.
I Samuel 10.24

And Agag[24] came unto him delicately.
I Samuel 15.32

Now he [David] was ruddy, and withal of a beautiful countenance, and goodly to look to.
I Samuel 16.12

How are the mighty fallen! Tell it not in Gath, publish it not in the streets of Ashkelon.
II Samuel 1.19-20

Then said his wife unto him [Job], Curse God, and die!
Job 2.9

Man is born unto trouble, as the sparks fly upward.
Job 5.7

I am escaped with the skin of my teeth.
Job 19.20

The price of wisdom is above rubies.
Job 28.18

Go to the ant, thou sluggard: consider her ways, and be wise.

Proverbs 6.6

Hope deferred maketh the heart sick.

Proverbs 13.12

He that spareth the rod hateth his son: but he that loveth him chasteneth him betimes.

Proverbs 13.24

Pride goeth before destruction, and a haughty spirit before a fall.

Proverbs 16.18

Vanity of vanities, saith the Preacher, vanity of vanities: all is vanity. What profit hath a man of all his labour which he taketh under the sun?

Ecclesiastes 1.2-3

As the crackling of thorns under a pot, so is the laughter of the fool.

Ecclesiastes 7.6

I commended mirth, because a man hath no better thing under the sun than to eat, and to drink, and to be merry: for that shall abide with him of his labour the days of his life, which God giveth him under the sun.

Ecclesiastes 8.15

I returned, and saw under the sun, that the race is not to the swift, nor the battle to the strong ... but time and chance happeneth to them all.

Ecclesiastes 9.11

And further, by these, my son, be admonished: of making many books there is no end; and much study is a weariness of the flesh.

Ecclesiasticus 12.12

Come now, and let us reason together, saith the Lord. Though thy sins be as scarlet, they shall be as white as snow: though they be red like crimson, they shall be as wool.

Isaiah 1.18

What mean ye that ye beat my people to pieces, and grind the faces of the poor? saith the Lord God.

Isaiah 3.15

Let us eat and drink: for tomorrow we die.

Isaiah 22.13

Can the Ethiopian change his skin, or the leopard his spots? Jeremiah 13.23

The fathers have eaten sour grapes, and the children's teeth are set on edge.

Ezekiel 18.2

Belshazzar the king[25] made a great feast to a thousand of his lords, and drank wine before the thousand ... In the same hour came forth fingers of a man's hand, and wrote over against the candlestick upon the plaster of the wall of the king's palace: and the king saw the part of the hand that wrote ... And this is the writing that was written: Mene, Mene, Tekel, Upharsin. This is the interpretation of the thing: Mene: God hath numbered thy kingdom, and finished it. Tekel: thou art weighed in the balance and found wanting. Peres: Thy kingdom is divided, and given to the Medes and Persians.[26]

Daniel 5.1,5,25-28

Then the king [Darius I of Persia, 521-486 BC] commanded, and they brought Daniel, and cast him into the den of lions ... Then said Daniel unto the king, O king, live for ever. My God hath sent his angel, and hath shut the lions' mouths, and they have not hurt me.[27]

Daniel 6.16,21-22

Judge none blessed before his death.

Ecclesiasticus 11.28

He that touches pitch shall be defiled therewith.

Ecclesiasticus 13.1

Let us now praise famous men, and our fathers that begat us ... Their bodies are buried in peace: but their name liveth for evermore. Ecclesiasticus 44.1

PART II

THE NEW TESTAMENT

The Kingship of God

In those days came John the Baptist, preaching in the wilderness of Judaea, and saying: Repent ye: for the kingdom of heaven is at hand.   Matthew 3.1-2

Blessed are the poor in spirit: for theirs is the kingdom of heaven.   Matthew 5.3

Watch therefore: for ye know not what hour your Lord doth come.   Matthew 24.42

The time is fulfilled, and the Kingdom of God is at hand: repent ye, and believe the Gospel.   Mark 1.15

Suffer the little children to come unto me, and forbid them not: for of such is the Kingdom of God.

Mark 10.14

Verily I say unto you, that this generation shall not pass, till all these things be done.   Mark 13.30

Let your loins be girded about, and your lights burning.

Luke 12.35

The Kingdom of God is within you.   Luke 17.21[28]

Verily, verily, I say unto you, the hour is coming, and now is, when the dead shall hear the voice of the Son of God: and they that hear shall live.   John 5.25

But this I say, brethren, the time is short.
                                        I Corinthians 7.29

Christ the firstfruits: afterwards they that are Christ's at his coming. Then cometh the end, when he shall have delivered up the Kingdom to God, even the Father ... The last enemy that shall be destroyed is death.
                                        I Corinthians 15.23-24,26

Therefore if any man be in Christ, he is a new creature: old things are passed away: behold, all things are become new.   II Corinthians 5.17

Yourselves know perfectly that the day of the Lord so cometh as a thief in the night.
                                        I Thessalonians 5.2

The Lord Jesus shall be revealed from heaven with his mighty angels, in flaming fire taking vengeance on them that know not God, and that obey not the Gospel of our Lord Jesus Christ.   II Thessalonians 1.7-8

I charge thee therefore before God, and the Lord Jesus Christ, who shall judge the quick and the dead at his appearing and his kingdom.   II Timothy 4.1

For yet a little while, and he that shall come will come, and will not tarry.   Hebrews 10.37

Be ye also patient: stablish your hearts: for the coming of the Lord draweth nigh.   James 5.8

Little children, it is the last time.   I John 2.18

The time is at hand ... Behold, I come quickly: and my reward is with me, to give every man according as his work shall be.
                                        Revelation 22.10,12

Satan[29]

Then saith Jesus unto him, Get thee hence, Satan! For it is written, Thou shalt worship the Lord thy God, and him only shalt thou serve.

Matthew 4.10

The Pharisees said, This fellow doth not cast out devils, but by Beelzebub the prince of devils.

Matthew 12.24

And he said unto them, I beheld Satan as lightning fall from heaven.

Luke 10.18

And the Lord said, Simon, Simon [Peter], behold, Satan hath desired to have you, that he may sift you as wheat.

Luke 22.31

But Peter said, Ananias,[30] why hath Satan filled thy heart to lie to the Holy Ghost, and keep back part of the price of the land.

Acts 5.3

The God of peace shall bruise Satan under your feet shortly.

Romans 16.20

What concord hath Christ with Belial?[31]

II Corinthians 6.15

In time past ye walked according to the course of this world, according to the prince of the power of the air, the spirit that now worketh in the children of disobedience.

Ephesians 2.2

Neither give place to the devil.

Ephesians 4.27

Put on the whole armour of God, that ye may be able to stand against the wiles of the devil.

Ephesians 6.11

Forasmuch then as the children are partakers of flesh and blood, he also himself likewise took part of the same: that through death he might destroy him that had the power of death, that is, the devil.

Hebrews 2.14

Resist the devil, and he will flee from you.

James 4.7

Be sober, be vigilant: because your adversary the devil, as a roaring lion, walketh about, seeking whom he may devour.

I Peter 5.8

And the great dragon was cast out, that old serpent, called the Devil, and Satan, which deceiveth the whole world: he was cast out into the earth, and his angels were cast out with him.

Revelation 12.9

And the devil that deceived them was cast into the lake of fire and brimstone, where the beast and the false prophet are, and shall be tormented day and night for ever and ever.

Revelation 20.10

The Jews & the Law

And he [Jesus] opened his mouth, and taught them, saying – Think not that I am come to destroy the Law, or the prophets: I am come not to destroy, but to fulfil.

Matthew 5.1,17

Then spake Jesus to the multitude, and to his disciples, saying – Woe unto you, scribes[32] and Pharisees,[33] hypocrites! For ye are like unto whited sepulchres,[34] which indeed appear beautiful outward, but are within full of dead men's bones, and of all uncleanness.

Matthew 23.1,25

Now do ye Pharisees make clean the outside of the cup and platter: but your inward part is full of ravening and wickedness.

Luke 11.39

And the Pharisees and scribes murmured, saying, This man receiveth sinners, and eateth with them.

Luke 15.2

And he [Jesus] said unto them – The Law and the prophets were until John [the Baptist]: since that time the Kingdom of God is preached.

Luke 16.15,16

For the law of the spirit of life in Christ Jesus hath made me free of the law of sin and death.

Romans 8.2

Christ is the end of the Law for righteousness to everyone that believeth.

Romans 10.4

If righteousness come by the Law, then Christ is dead in vain.

Galatians 2.21

Christ hath redeemed us from the curse of the Law.

Galatians 3.13

The Law was our schoolmaster to bring us unto Christ, that we might be justified by faith. But after that faith is come, we are no longer under a schoolmaster.

Galatians 3.24-25

Behold, I Paul say unto you, that if ye be circumcised, Christ shall profit you nothing.

Galatians 5.2

All the Law is fulfilled in one word, even in this: Thou shalt love thy neighbour as thyself.

Galatians 5.14

Non-Jews: Foreigners

When Jesus heard it, he marvelled, and said to them that
followed: Verily I say unto you, I have not found so
great faith, no not in Israel.[35]   Matthew 8.10

These twelve Jesus sent forth, and commanded them,
saying – Go not into the way of the Gentiles,[36] and into
any city of the Samaritans[37] enter ye not: but go rather to
the lost sheep of the house of Israel.

Matthew 10.5

Verily I say unto you, no prophet is accepted in his own
country.   Luke 4.24

A certain man went down from Jerusalem to Jericho,
and fell among thieves, which stripped him of his
raiment, and wounded him, and departed, leaving him
half dead. And by chance there came down a certain
priest that way: and when he saw him, he passed by on
the other side. And likewise a Levite,[38] when he was at
the place, came and looked on him, and passed by on the
other side. But a certain Samaritan,[39] as he journeyed,
came where he was, and when he saw him, he had
compassion on him. And went to him, and bound his
wounds, pouring in oil and wine, and set him on his
own beast, and brought him to an inn, and took care of
him.[40]   Luke 10.30-34

Then saith the woman of Samaria unto him, How is it
that thou, being a Jew, askest drink of me, which am a
woman of Samaria? For the Jews have no dealings with
the Samaritans.   John 4.9

Then Paul and Barnabas[41] waxed bold, and said, It was
necessary that the word of God should first have been
spoken to you [the Jews]; but seeing ye put it from you,
and judge yourself unworthy of everlasting life, lo, we
turn to the Gentiles.   Acts 13.46

All they which dwelt in Asia heard the word of the Lord
Jesus, both Jews and Greeks ... Ye see and hear, that not
alone at Ephesus, but almost throughout all Asia, this
Paul hath persuaded and turned away much people,
saying that they be no gods which are made by hands.

Acts 19.10,26

Be it known therefore unto you that the salvation of God
is sent unto the Gentiles, and that they will hear it. And
when he had said these words, the Jews departed, and
had great reasoning among themselves.

Acts 28.28-29

Glory, honour and peace to every man that worketh
good, to the Jew first, and also to the Gentile. For there is
no respect of persons with God.   Romans 2.10-11

For there is no difference between the Jew and the
Greek: for the same Lord over all is rich unto all that call
upon him.   Romans 10.12

It pleased God ... to reveal his Son in me, that I might
preach him among the heathen.

Galatians 1.16

They saw that the Gospel of the uncircumcision[42] was
committed unto me, as the Gospel of the circumcision
was to Peter ... But when Peter was come to Antioch, I
withstood him to the face, because he was to be blamed.

Galatians 2.7,11

Unto me, who am less than the least of all the saints,[43] is
this grace given, that I should preach among the Gentiles
the unsearchable riches of Christ.   Ephesians 3.8

Ye have put on the new man ... where there is neither
Greek nor Jew, circumcision nor uncircumcision,
barbarian, Scythian,[44] bond nor free: but Christ is all, and
in all.   Colossians 3.10,11

Conversion

And Jesus, walking by the sea of Galilee, saw two
brethren, Simon called Peter, and Andrew his brother,
casting a net into the sea: for they were fishers. And he
saith unto them: Follow me. And I will make you fishers
of men.

Matthew 4.18-19

Verily I say unto you, Except ye be converted, and
become as little children, ye shall not enter into the
Kingdom of Heaven.

Matthew 18.3

And with many other words did he [Peter] testify and
exhort, saying, Save yourselves from this untoward
generation. Then they that had gladly received his word
were baptized: and the same day there were added unto
them about three thousand souls.

Acts 2.40-41

And it came to pass that, as I made my journey, and was
come nigh unto Damascus about noon, suddenly there
shone from heaven a great light round about me.[45] And I
fell unto the ground, and heard a voice saying unto me,
Saul, Saul, why persecutest thou me?

Acts 22.67-7

At that time ye were without Christ ... But now in Christ
Jesus ye who sometimes were far off are made nigh by
the blood of Christ. Ephesians 2.13

And ye became followers of us, and of the Lord, having
received the word in much affliction, with joy of the
Holy Ghost.

I Thessalonians 1.6

Faith

Daughter,[46] be of good comfort: thy faith hath made thee whole.

Matthew 9.22

Then Jesus answered and said unto her, O woman,[47] great is thy faith. Be it unto thee even as thou wilt! And her daughter was made whole from that very hour.

Matthew 15.28

Verily, I say unto you, if you have faith and doubt not … if ye shall say unto this mountain, be thou removed, and be thou cast into the sea: it shall be done.

Matthew 21.21

As it is written, the just shall live by faith.

Romans 1.17

Your faith should not stand in the wisdom of men, but in the power of God.

I Corinthians 2.5

Fight the good fight of faith.

I Timothy 6.12

Through faith we understand that the worlds were framed by the word of God.

Hebrews 11.3

What doth it profit, my brethren, though a man say he hath faith, and have not works? Can faith save him?

James 2.14

Forgiveness

Resist not evil: but whosoever shall smite thee on thy right cheek, turn to him the other also.

Matthew 5.39

If ye forgive men their trespasses, your heavenly Father will also forgive you.   Matthew 6.14

Then came Peter to him and said, Lord, how oft shall my brother sin against me, and I forgive him? Till seven times? Jesus saith unto him, I say not unto thee, Until seven times: but until seventy times seven.

Matthew 18.21-22

And, as they were eating, Jesus took bread, and blessed it, and brake it, and gave it to the disciples, and said, Take, eat: this is my body. And he took the cup, and gave thanks, and gave it to them, saying, Drink ye all of it: for this is my blood of the new testament, which is shed for many for the remission of sins.[48]

Matthew 26.26-28

But there were certain of the scribes sitting there, and reasoning in their hearts: Why doth this man thus speak blasphemies? Who can forgive sins but God only?

Mark 2.6-7

Love your enemies, do good to them that hate you.[49] Bless them that curse you, and pray for them which despitefully use you.

Luke 6.27-28

Her sins, which are many, are forgiven, for she loved much: but to whom little is forgiven, the same loveth little. And he said unto her, Thy sins are forgiven. And they that sat at meat with him began to say within themselves, Who is this that forgiveth sins also?

Luke 7.47-49

Father, forgive them: for they know not what they do.

Luke 23.34

And you, being dead in your sins and the uncircum-cision of your flesh, hath he [Jesus] quickened together with him, having forgiven you all trespasses.

Colossians 2.13

Crucifixion & Resurrection

And Jesus stood before the governor [Pontius Pilate], and the governor asked him, saying, Art thou the King of the Jews? And Jesus said to him, *Thou* sayest.[51]

Matthew 27.11

And the governor said, Why, what evil hath he done? But they cried out the more, saying, let him be crucified.

Matthew 27.23

And at the ninth hour Jesus cried with a loud voice, saying, Eloi, Eloi, lama sabachthani? which is, being interpreted: My God, my God, why hast thou forsaken me?

Mark 15.34

And the sun was darkened, and the veil of the temple was rent in the midst.

Luke 23.45

[Christ Jesus] whom God hath set forth to be a propitiation through faith in his blood, to declare his righteousness for the remission of sins that are past, through the forbearance of God.

Romans 3.25

Know ye not, that so many of us as were baptized unto Jesus Christ were baptized unto his death? ... that like as Christ was raised up from the dead by the glory of the Father, even so we should also walk in newness of life.

Romans 6.4

We preach Christ crucified, unto the Jews a stumbling-block, and unto the Greeks foolishness.

I Corinthians 1.23

For I determined not to know anything among you, save Jesus Christ, and him crucified.

I Corinthians 2.2

If Christ be not risen, then is our preaching vain, and your faith is also vain.

I Corinthians 15.14

But some man will say, How are the dead raised up? And with what body do they come? ... The resurrection of the dead is sown in corruption: it is raised in incorruption ... It is sown a natural body; it is raised a spiritual body.[52]

I Corinthians 15.35,42,44

Redemption

For even the Son of Man[53] came not to be ministered unto, but to minister, and to give his life a ransom for many.

Mark 10.45

Your redemption draweth nigh.

Luke 21.28

For ye are bought with a price.

I Corinthians 6.20; 7.23

Lord Jesus Christ gave himself for our sins, that he might deliver us from this present evil world, according to the will of God and our Father.[54]

Galatians 1.4

Stand fast therefore in the liberty wherewith Christ has made us free, and be not entangled again with the yoke of bondage.

Galatians 5.1

In whom we have redemption through his blood, the forgiveness of sins, according to the riches of his grace.

Ephesians 1.7

Forasmuch as ye know that ye were not redeemed with corruptible things, as silver and gold, from your vain conversation received by tradition from your fathers: but with the precious blood of Christ, as of a lamb without blemish and without spot.

I Peter 1.18

Thou wast slain, and hast redeemed us to God by thy blood, out of every kindred, and tongue, and people, and nation.

Revelation 5.9

Women

The angel of the Lord appeared unto him in a dream,
saying Joseph, thou son of David, fear not to take unto
thee Mary thy wife: for that which is conceived in her is
of the Holy Ghost. And she shall bring forth a son.[55]

Matthew 1.20-21

And the angel came in unto her, and said, Hail, thou that
art highly favoured. The Lord is with thee: blessed art
thou among women. ... And Mary said; My soul doth
magnify the Lord: and my spirit hath rejoiced in God my
saviour.

Luke 1.28,46-47

There came then his brethren and his mother, and,
standing without, sent unto him, calling him. And the
multitude sat about him, and they said unto him,
Behold, thy mother and thy brethren without seek for
thee. And he answered them, saying: Who is my mother,
or my brethren? And he looked round about on them
which sat about him, and said, Behold my mother and
my brethren! For whosoever shall do the will of God, the
same is my brother, and my sister, and my mother.

Mark 3.31-35

And they twain [husband and wife] shall be one flesh: so
then they are no more twain, but one flesh. What
therefore God hath joined together, let not man put
asunder.[56]

Mark 10.8-9

There were also women looking on afar off: among whom was Mary Magdalene, and Mary the mother of James the Less and of Joses [Joseph], and Salome ... And when the sabbath was past, [they] had brought sweet spices, so that they might come and anoint him ... And they said among themselves, Who shall roll us away the stone from the door of the sepulchre? And when they looked, they saw that the stone was rolled away: for it was very great ... Now when Jesus was risen early the first day of the week, he appeared first to Mary Magdalene, out of whom he had cast seven devils.

Mark 15.40; 16.3-4,9

I commend unto you Phebe our sister, which is a servant of the church which is at Cenchreae:[57] that ye receive her in the Lord, as becometh saints, and that ye assist her in whatsoever business she hath need of you: for she hath been a succourer of many, and of myself also.

Romans 16.1-2

I say therefore to the unmarried and widows, it is good for them if they abide even as I. But if they cannot contain, let them marry: for it is better to marry than to burn.

I Corinthians 7.8-9

Wives, submit yourselves unto your husbands, as unto the Lord ... Husbands, love your wives, even as Christ also loved the church, and gave himself for it.

Ephesians 5.22,25

Whoremongers and adulterers God will judge.

Hebrews 13.4

The Poor[58]

If thou wilt be perfect, go and sell that thou hast, and
give to the poor.

Matthew 19.21

It is easier for a camel to go through the eye of a needle
than for a rich man to enter into the kingdom of God.

Matthew 19.24

When thou makest a feast, call the poor, the maimed, the
lame, the blind.

Luke 14.13

But Abraham said, Son, remember that thou in thy
lifetime receivedst thy good things, and likewise Lazarus
evil things: but now he is comforted, and thou art
tormented.

Luke 16.25

Only they would that we should remember the poor: the
same which I also was forward to do.

Galatians 2.10

For we brought nothing into the world, and it is certain
that we can carry nothing out.

I Timothy 6.7

But ye have despised the poor.

James 2.6

Slaves & Masters[59]

Servants, be obedient to them that are your masters according to the flesh, with fear and trembling, in singleness of your heart, as unto Christ ... knowing that whatsoever good thing any man doeth, the same shall be he receive of the Lord, whether he be bond or free ... There is no respect of persons with him.

Ephesians 6.5,8-9

Servants, obey in all things your masters according to the flesh; not with eye-service, as men-pleasers; but in singleness of heart, fearing God. And whatsoever ye do, do it heartily, as to the Lord, and not unto men.

Colossians 3.22-23

Let as many servants as are under the yoke count their own masters worthy of all honour, that the name of God and his doctrine be not blasphemed.

I Timothy 6.1

If you count me therefore a partner, receive him [the slave Onesimus][60] as myself. If he hath wronged thee, or oweth thee ought, put that on mine account.

Philemon 17-18

Shocks & Surprises

And he said unto them [the devils], Go! And when they were come out, they went into the herd of swine: and behold, the whole herd of swine ran violently down a steep place into the sea, and perished in the waters.

Matthew 8.32

I came not to send peace, but a sword.

Matthew 10.34

And Jesus went into the temple of God, and cast out all them that sold and bought in the temple, and overthrew the tables of the money-changers, and the seats of them that sold doves.

Matthew 21.12

And when he saw a fig tree in the way, he came to it, and found nothing thereon, but leaves only, and said unto it, Let no fruit grow on thee henceforward for ever. And presently the fig tree withered away.

Matthew 21.19

Jesus said unto him [Peter]: Verily I say unto thee, that this night, before the cock crow, thou shalt deny me thrice. Peter said unto him: Though I should die with thee, yet shall I not deny thee! [But he denies him three times: this was the third.] Then began he to curse and to swear, saying, I know not the man. And immediately the cock crew ... And he went out, and wept bitterly.

Matthew 26.34-35,74-75

And the third day there was a marriage in Cana of Galilee ... And when they wanted wine, the mother of Jesus saith unto him, They have no wine. ... Jesus saith unto them, Fill the waterpots with water. And they filled them up to the brim ... The ruler of the feast tasted the water, that was made wine, and knew not whence it was.

John 2.1,3,7,9

Famous Epigrams & Bywords

Now when Jesus was born in Bethlehem[61] of Judaea in the days of Herod the King, behold, there came wise men from the east to Jerusalem, saying, Where is he that is born King of the Jews? For we have seen his star in the east, and are come to worship him. *Matthew 2.1-2*

Man shall not live by bread alone, but by every word that proceedeth out of the mouth of God.

Matthew 4.4

Ye are the salt of the earth; but if the salt have lost his savour, wherewith shall it be salted? *Matthew 5.13*

No man can serve two masters ... Ye cannot serve God and Mammon. *Matthew 6.24*

And why take ye thought for raiment? Consider the lilies of the field, how they grow; they toil not, neither do they spin: and yet I say unto you, that even Solomon in all his glory was not arrayed like one of these.

Matthew 6.28-29

Take therefore no thought for the morrow: for the morrow shall take thought for the things of itself. Sufficient unto the day is the evil thereof.

Matthew 6.34

Judge not, that ye be not judged. *Matthew 7.1*

Thou hypocrite, first cast out the beam out of thine own eye; and then shalt thou see clearly to cast out the mote out of thy brother's eye. *Matthew 7.5*

Neither cast ye your pearls before swine, lest they trample them under their feet, and turn again and rend you.

Matthew 7.6

Strait is the gate, and narrow is the way, which leadeth
unto life, and few there be that find it.   Matthew 7.14

Come unto me, all ye that labour and are heavy laden,
and I will give you rest.   Matthew 11.28

A prophet is not without honour, save in his own
country, and in his own house.   Matthew 13.57

For what is a man profited, if he shall gain the whole
world, and lose his own soul?   Matthew 16.26

But many that are first shall be last; and the last shall be
first.   Matthew 19.30

For many are called, but few are chosen.
                                               Matthew 22.14

Show me the tribute money. And they brought him a
penny. And he saith unto them, Whose is this image and
superscription? They say unto him, Caesar's.[62] Then
saith he unto them, Render therefore unto Caesar the
things that are Caesar's; and unto God the things that
are God's.   Matthew 22.19-21

Heaven and earth shall pass away; but my words shall
not pass away.   Matthew 24.35

Watch and pray, that ye enter not into temptation; the
spirit indeed is willing, but the flesh is weak.
                                               Matthew 26.41

All they that take the sword shall perish with the sword.
                                               Matthew 26.52

And no man putteth new wine into old bottles: else the
new wine doth burst the bottles, and the wine is spilled,
and the bottles will be marred; but new wine must be
put into new bottles.   Mark 2.22

And he said unto them, The sabbath was made for man,
and not man for the sabbath.   Mark 2.27

And he said unto them, He that hath ears to hear, let him
hear.   Mark 4.9

Physician, heal thyself.

                                                   Luke 4.23

He that is not with me is against me.

                                                   Luke 11.23

Rise, take up thy bed, and walk.

                                                   John 5.8

He that believeth on me hath everlasting life.

                                                   John 6.47

The poor always ye have with you; but me ye have not
always.

                                                   John 12.8

Greater love hath no man than this, that a man lay down
his life for his friends.

                                                   John 15.13

It is hard for thee to kick against the pricks.[63]

                                                   Acts 9.5

All with one voice about the space of two hours cried
out, Great is Diana of the Ephesians![64]

                                                   Acts 19.34

He said, It is more blessed to give than to receive.

                                                   Acts 20.35

The wages of sin is death.

                                                   Romans 6.23

The good that I would I do not; but the evil which I
would not, that I do.

                                                   Romans 7.19

O death, where is thy sting? O grave, where is thy
victory?

                                                   I Corinthians 15.55

There was given me [Paul] a thorn in the flesh,[65] the messenger of Satan to buffet me, lest I should be exalted above measure.

II Corinthians 12.7

We brought nothing into the world, and it is certain we can carry nothing out.

I Timothy 6.7

It is a fearful thing to fall into the hands of the living God.

Hebrews 10.31

Whom the Lord loveth he chasteneth.

Hebrews 12.6

If we say that we have no sin, we deceive ourselves, and the truth is not in us.

I John 1.8

I am Alpha and Omega, the beginning and the ending, saith the Lord.[66]

Revelation 1.8

Notes

1. See M. Grant, *History of Ancient Israel*, index, s.v.

2. For their dates, M. Grant, *Jesus*, pp. 183ff.

3. M. Grant, *Saint Paul*, pp. 4ff.

4. For this mysterious saying see M. Grant, *History of Ancient Israel*, p. 45: I am; that is who I am; I am the one who is; whose essentially unchangeable continuity can be seen at all times. *Or* (since Hebrew lacks the tenses of Indo-European tongues) I shall be what I shall be.

5. 'Unfurled the skies by his understanding' (New English Bible).

6. 'She got a rush basket for him, made it watertight with clay and tar, laid him in it, and put it among the reeds by the bank of the Nile' (New English Bible).

7. Joshua's miraculous conquest of Jericho opened up the Holy Land to him.

8. The pagan god of the Canaanites.

9. These are some of the principal Old Testament texts which Christians later believed to have prefigured the coming and crucifixion of Jesus.

10. *Bar nasha* in Aramaic: a term later applied to Jesus. For its various meanings see G.B. Caird, *Saint Luke* (1963), p. 94.

11. A nomad tribe which although related to the Israelites cooperated with Moab against Israel.

12. A Jew who lived at Bethlehem: ancestor of David.

13. Judith was a Jew, and Holofernes a general serving Nebuchadnezzar (Nebuchadrezzar II), who is called King of Assyria instead of Babylon, where he, in fact, ruled (605-562 BC).

14. A country in south-eastern Palestine, centred upon Mount Seir.

15. The Ten Commandments.

16. King of Israel (*c.* 871-852 BC).

17. 'Your sandalled feet' (New English Bible).

18. 'That shall never want for spiced wine' (New English Bible).

19. Ham (father of Canaan) saw his father Noah in this condition, and Noah, discovering this, cursed Canaan: slave of slaves shall he be to his brothers (Shem and Japheth).

20. Jacob deceived his blind father by wearing goat-skins so

that he would seem to be his hairy brother Esau, and receive the firstborn's blessing.

21. David wanted Uriah's wife Bathsheba. Joab was David's nephew and commander-in-chief.

22. An Israelite centre of pilgrimage, ten miles north of Jerusalem.

23. A Canaanite general killed by Jael, the wife of Heber the Kenite.

24. An Amalekite king spared by Saul but cut to pieces by Samuel.

25. According to other sources Belshazzar was the viceroy of Nabonidus, the last king of Babylon (556-539 BC).

26. The literal translation is generally accepted as: It has been counted and counted, weighed and cut up.

27. Most modern critics believe that these stories were composed in *c.* 300 (and/or 165) BC. Some maintain that 'Daniel' is derived from the wise and just sage mentioned in conjunction with Noah and Job in Ezekiel 14.14; cf. 28.3. Chapters 2.4-7.8 of Daniel are in Aramaic.

28. For another passage from Luke, referring to the Kingdom, see also the section on The Jews and the Law.

29. The ancient Jews, being monotheists, did *not* hold the dualist belief that God and Satan are the powers of good and evil warring for the dominance of the universe. 'Satan', in the Old Testament, is the transliteration of a Hebrew word for 'adversary', whose task was to roam round the earth seeking out acts or persons to be reported upon adversely: as Job had shown, he was permitted to test human goodness under God's authority and control and within the limits God sets. But in the New Testament he became the devil-prince of evil spirits, the inveterate enemy of God and of Christ. Under Iranian influence, old dualistic formulas are used, although Christian dogma repeatedly condemned dualism. Now, in the twentieth century, some have found it an attractive explanation of the horrors of our own age.

30. Ananias was a member of the first Christian community who, with his wife Sapphira, was allegedly punished by Peter with sudden death for falsehood.

31. Belial, a term applied to subversive individuals, was often synonymous with Satan.

32. 'Lawyers' (New English Bible). Ecclesiasticus had depicted the scribe as the literate man, occupied in particular with the study of the Jewish Law.

33. For this Jewish cultural élite, who called themselves 'Haberim' (equals), see M. Grant, *History of Ancient Israel*, pp. 216f. 'Pharisee' comes from a word meaning 'separated', indicating their intention to withdraw from everything sinful or unclean.

34. Tombs covered with whitewash (New English Bible).

35. This was when he supposedly healed the centurion (officer of the army) at Capernaum in Galilee.

36. Persons not of Jewish race.

37. These were people centred upon Samaria (near Shechem), the ancient capital of the kingdom of Israel, descended from the tribes of Ephraim and Manasseh – with an admixture of non-Israelite colonists – whose brand of Judaism (based on a variant of the Torah) was not, and is not, accepted by orthodox Jews (cf. John 4.9: 'The Jews have no dealings with the Samaritans'). Moses is the only prophet accepted by the Samaritans.

38. The Levites were descendants of the tribe of Levi, consecrated by Moses to serve as priests and teach the Torah in the Temple.

39. See note 37.

40. Jesus concludes that this person, though a Samaritan, was the true neighbour of the lawyer who asked: 'Who is my neighbour?'

41. The most important early Christian apostle to the Gentiles with the exception of Paul.

42. i.e. of the Gentiles, who did not practise the Jewish ritual of circumcision (*milah*, the cutting away of the foreskin).

43. 'Of all God's people' (New English Bible).

44. Scythia was the vast hinterland north of the Black Sea.

45. This is the psychological experience known as *photism*, discussed in M. Grant, *Saint Paul*, pp. 105-108. 'Saul' was Paul's Jewish name before he became a Roman citizen.

46. This was a woman who had suffered from an issue of blood (haemorrhage) for twelve years.

47. A Canaanite woman whose daughter was 'grievously vexed with a devil'.

48. This is my blood, the blood of the covenant, shed for many for the forgiveness of sins (New English Bible).

49. Regarded by orthodox Jews as a preposterous doctrine, because it was plainly unrealisable, M. Buber, *Two Types of Faith*, p. 68. But for the Jewish doctrines of forgiveness see above, Old Testament, section on Vengeance.

50. No Old Testament writer had suggested that God loves the sinner before he repents, and John the Baptist and Jesus probably likewise believed that repentance should come before forgiveness. (To Paul, however, the expiatory death of Jesus eliminates the idea of God's free forgiveness for the penitent sinner: since the Crucifixion has brought forgiveness already.)

51. 'The words are yours', *or* 'It is as you say' (New English Bible).

52. For earlier Jewish ideas about the resurrection of the dead, see M. Grant, *Jesus*, pp. 177 f.

53. The Old Testament background of this designation has already been mentioned (see the section on Prophets). For its meaning in connexion with Jesus, see M. Grant, *Jesus*, pp. 102 ff.

54. For the fundamental Christian belief that Jesus 'died to save us all', ibid., index, s.v. redemption.

55. Matthew and Luke insert the story of the Virgin Birth of Jesus, which Matthew interprets as the fulfilment of Isaiah 7.14, 'the virgin (*parthenos*) will conceive and bear a son'. But in the original Hebrew (cf New English Bible), the word had only meant 'young woman'.

56. This is a part of a wider discussion of the question of divorce.

57. Near Corinth.

58. When Jesus speaks of 'poor people' (*ptochoi*) he is sometimes referring to the 'poor in spirit' (e.g. Matthew 5.3 against Luke 6.20) – two terms which had already been closely associated in the Old Testament (e.g. *Psalms* 86.1 f, 132.15 f). See also the section on The Kingship of God.

59. For the Christian attitude to slavery, see L. Archer, *Slavery and Other Forms of Unfree Labour*, pp. 29 ff, 64, 122-6, 269 f.

60. The principal purpose of this letter is to persuade a certain Philemon to forgive and receive back his slave Onesimus, who had apparently run away.

61. It is more probable that Jesus was born in Galilee, M. Grant, *Jesus*, p. 72

62. i.e. the Roman emperor's. He was Tiberius (AD 14-37).

63. Omitted from the New English Bible.

64. The craftsmen who made silver models of the temple of Artemis (Diana) at Ephesus in Western Asia Minor objected to the preaching of Paul, which they believed would be bad for their trade.

65. What was Paul's trouble? A physical ailment, or sexual difficulties? M. Grant, *Saint Paul*, p. 25.

66. 'Who is and who was and is to come, the sovereign Lord of all' (New English Bible).